PILGRIM

PILGRIM

A Message To The Generation About To Inherit Their Country: Pilgrims In A New Land

Clark Cumings-Johnson

Copyright © 2024 by Clark Cumings-Johnson.

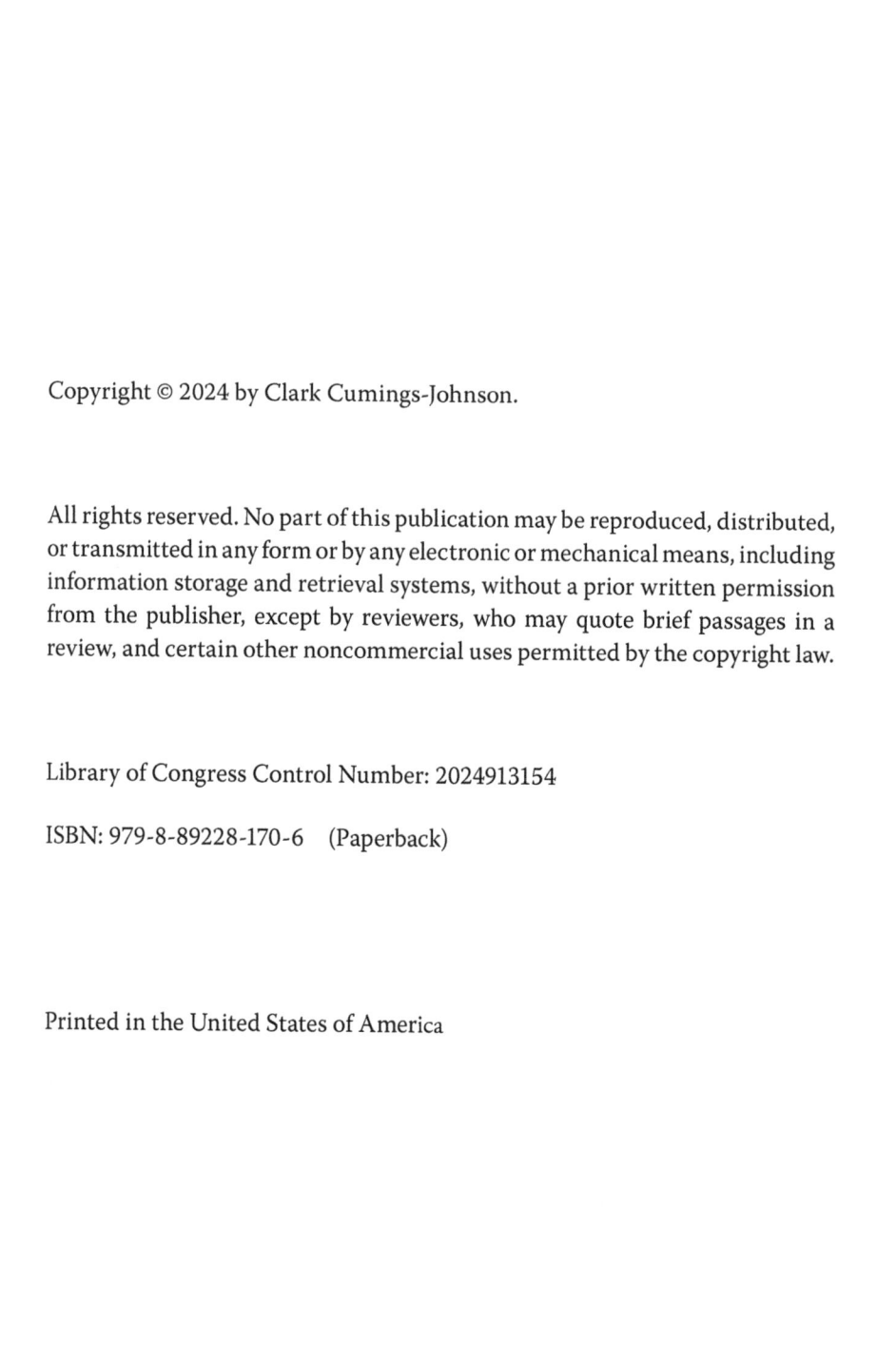

All rights reserved. No part of this publication may be reproduced, distributed, or transmitted in any form or by any electronic or mechanical means, including information storage and retrieval systems, without a prior written permission from the publisher, except by reviewers, who may quote brief passages in a review, and certain other noncommercial uses permitted by the copyright law.

Library of Congress Control Number: 2024913154

ISBN: 979-8-89228-170-6   (Paperback)

Printed in the United States of America

Author information is readily available online by Googling: Clark Cumings-Johnson.

This book is dedicated to the Post America generations.

Table Of Contents

Introduction xi

I	The Congress	1
II	The President	5
III	The Supreme Court	9
IV	Education	19
V	Economics	27
VI	Crime	41
VII	Divorce	45
VIII	Medical Science	51
IX	Sex And Gender	61
X	Population	73
XI	WW III	77

INTRODUCTION

Young people coming along today could be headed for the junk yard of human wreckage. Among their numbers will be legions of the walking dead who are not going anywhere except perhaps onto welfare and into government housing. This calamity is not their fault. But our failure to recognize and do something about the situation is. They are in effect Pilgrims in a new world not of their own making much as those who came to settle these shores.

For those who are offended by what follows are the ones likely to benefit most from the message offered. At the same time, it is the others who will be most apt to finish it. Please know I am interested in all of you and your thoughts.

This book is comprised of a series of scenarios. It was not written to please or entertain you. Its purpose is to inform you. It may even save your life, your future, socially and career-wise, as well as biologically via snapshots of reality.

Where to start was a challenge. Sociopolitical insights have been selected first to set the stage. Chapters which follow are topically presented. Some chapters are long, some short. Their order or length do not carry any implied message or weight.

On occasion an asterisk will appear following a term in the text. This signifies the reader is directed to the internet to learn more about the subject matter with which the term or title deals. This outside investigation is incorporated by reference and considered to be a part of this book.

Clark Cumings-Johnson

YOUR GOVERNMENT:

I

CONGRESS

With regard to the issues listed below, what will Congress be doing about them in 2024?

Inter alia:

The national debt;
A Social Security system on its way to insolvency;
A failed public education system;
Obesity, diabetes, STDs and waves of endemic viruses and plagues;
Wavering, irresolute, unsustainable financial policy;
Crime, grift and 'insider trading*.'

Nothing.

Why not?

The answers range from incompetence to paralyzing political infighting and the avoidance of voter minefields, to an abject absence of statesmanship, fear of loss of power, to lost grift or outright corruption, many politicians being in the pockets of others and unable to properly act even if inclined to do so. Too few are truly free from such restraints and are unable to escape their political snares, or at least not enough for the country to enjoy the benefit of an effective legislative branch of government. At the same time don't think branches of state and local government are free from such disabilities.

The venal politicians get their cut and now must stay bought.

One hesitates to even think about getting into the bramble bush of any of the stated national problems with which Congress needs to grapple. Nevertheless, let us take a look. The easiest one to solve is likely Social Security even though it is the second largest political hot topic. Its solutions turn out to simply be a numbers game and an informed electorate. The results will affect you.

As it stands, politicians can't even say the words 'Social Security' out loud in public. When is the last time you heard your elected Representative say anything close to 'something needs to be done about the financing of Social Security' to prevent it from becoming bankrupt, or 'the longer Congress delays the greater the pain will be?'

It can be made a solvent program, but the pathway getting there could carry along with it some political detritus, and politicians are a fearful lot, but that depends. As a general matter, citizens know reform is needed if the system is to continue in any semblance of its present form. Coupled with this is the ability of the Congress to design a fair and rational preservation plan and to present it candidly and honestly to an informed electorate with a full explanation as to why it is necessary.

Number one, leave everyone now in the system just as they are making that point clear to them. Next, let the public know changes are being made so as to ensure the social security system will be preserved for future generations, an important point for both those in and coming into the system. Those already in the system want a solvent system for their children and those coming in want a solvent system and not one that will become insolvent before they get there or as they enter having come to depend upon it for their planning purposes.

Next, remove the cap on annual contributions for high income earners. How is it possible they could fairly complain about that? As it stands, they contribute nothing after a certain level of income, where everyone else below them continue to pay this ungraduated 'tax' throughout the year. It is blatantly regressive.

Then, so far as the very wealthy are concerned, a prorated setoff of benefits against income levels on a sliding scale even if it eliminates any social security retirement benefit is not only fair and rational, but acceptable by most who will be affected. Ask them, they will tell you so. There is no rational or fairness based complaint from those who are well settled and simply do not need anything added to their retirement.

Leave the eligibility for entry age the same, but prorate out the standards of "full age," full benefits and the schedule of increased benefits from delayed entry into the system consistent with modern actuarial tables.

Taken together, these simple changes would not only shore up the retirement component of social security but assist funding programs in place to assist the relatively few desperate citizens who have been visited with calamity in their lives.

Pretty simple, and don't try to make it out to be something it isn't. It is simple. And if it is designed fairly, based on publicly understood necessity with full disclosure, and presented in an open and honest way, it will overall come into being with political benefits, not costs.

So, why hasn't Congress fixed it? For the same reasons cited at the outset. But unfortunately, there is more. There are members of Congress who want to keep it as it is for political reasons. They need grist for the blame game mill. They want the 'heroic' mantle of adding a benefit for which very public credit will be taken when in reality it is only a 'thrown fish.' It wants the 'crisis' and will do everything to preserve it and not waste it with a cure. Members want to be able to use it as a political cudgel.

At base what you have observed is a lack of statesmanship coupled with uninformed voters being purposely kept in the dark, blind and stupid, the very vulnerabilities of the Republic to which Franklin and Jefferson spoke.

Will Congress act with regard to this?

No.

What will be the catalyst which will bring about change? Bankruptcy, financial collapse, or being on the brink thereof…, or a world war coming to our shores…, likely the latter happening first.

*

National debt? Same thing. I could go on, but I'll spare you. Anyway, you already know the answer.

Insider trading? Same.

Education, obesity, infectious disease, national fiscal irresponsibility?

Nothing rational will be done, its use for political capital left in place.

War with whom; other belligerent nations, or among ourselves? Both, the latter following the former.

This will not be a very good year.

Perhaps there is something you can do, Pilgrim?

II

THE PRESIDENT

What will the President do to help in 2024?

Nothing.

Nothing but piddling the country's way into a world war or behave in such a manner that it becomes inexorably inevitable.

Will nuclear weapons be used?

Yes.

Will the United States win?

No.

There will not be any winning nations in the conventional sense. However, there will be winners of sorts. Among the net results, obligations to nations holding U. S. debt deemed belligerent will be cancelled. Non-belligerents will get something less than full payment [in order to maintain some degree of 'healthy' business and international relations] which will include offsets for the expenses of their defense. The public side of the government's debt while not being apt to fully default rather will be 'reorganized' to a level that can be sustained [which will not be much]. The retirees will be hurt by far the most while benefits for health care will be revised and/or rationed, discussed *infra*, if following the next Great War the issue will even be relevant. The number of beneficiaries will be dramatically reduced as they predominantly live in population centers most likely to be eliminated.

All of this assumes that the present government survives or can reestablish itself in some meaningful way, *post bellum*.

At the same time summary executions of governmental wrongdoers from every branch along with their private counterparts taken from lists will become so common that in time only data will be reported, and then eventually only estimated data.

There are those who have been heard to say the present problems of debt, crime, education, social ills, cultural convulsions, to name just a few, will be instantly solved. Perhaps, but businesses will nevertheless immediately re-emerge influenced and organized by the natural forces of vertical and horizontal integration upon which free enterprise is based. Initially it will be self-policed.

Cities now in ruins of rubble will be abandoned and new ones begun. The remnants and detritus of war will give way to recovery and the remediation of nature. Elsewhere new cities will quickly begin to replace the former staggered, helter-skelter skylines of soul-less, faceless, unimaginative structures, the older ones of rock and stone now gutted standing as ghosts.

Race will no longer be in anyone's playbook. No one will suffer from gender confusion or misapprehension. What one knows and what one does will be determinative of what success one experiences. The seeds of a lost America will arise from the forest floor and again come to life. The Constitution will survive as it is in essence collective thinking. Lawfulness will be insisted upon in all dealings, in all conduct, not just financially, but personally and socially as well. Those who are sent to government will put the country ahead of themselves, a lesson of history now having been learned.

Some other countries may fare in a similar fashion, while many will not as they will cease to exist and their survivors becoming running dogs. Yet in time some existing nations will develop meaningful, cooperative, and productive interrelationships to maximize the value to their resources and wealth [See: Economics, *infra*] contributing to peace, trade, prosperity, and world order.

Hypothetically speaking, it is chilling to think one might look back and see that but for the incompetence and evil of national and international leaders, the new order would never have emerged. At the same time, the question becomes what course should now be elected to best serve the interests of all mankind?

Why not enter politics, Pilgrim?

III

THE SUPREME COURT

It could be fairly said that the case of Dobbs vs. Jackson, 597 U. S. 215 [or volume number 597 of the United States Supreme Court Reports, starting on page 215 (it, like most everything else, is available on-line by entering 597 U. S. 215*)] was among the most, if not the most significant development in American jurisprudence so far this decade, while Relentless, Inc. v. Department of Commerce, Docket Number 22-1219*, now pending before the High Court will set the jurisprudential high-water mark of the year if the Court manages to decide it this year which likely it will, but if not then next year.

[Note this book makes references to relevant portions of the Constitution of the United States and reported opinions of the High Court and incorporate same making them a part hereof for your review. As stated, they are, *inter alia*, part of the message.]

As you will recall, *Dobbs* is the Supreme Court opinion which returned jurisdiction over the issue of abortion back to the states after having previously taken jurisdiction in the case of Roe Vs. Wade, 410 U. S. 113. *Dobbs* concluded its opinion by stating the Constitution does not prohibit States from regulating abortion, such authority being vested in the people and their elected representatives. This result is consistent with the Tenth Amendment* as the Constitution is otherwise silent with regard to the matter. The *Roe* court had previously taken jurisdiction on a basis that the rights of "due process" provided for in the Fourteenth Amendment*, from which, *inter alia*, a "right of privacy" was gleaned, were violated by the Texas statute regulating abortion then in question before the High Court.

While the Fourteenth Amendment is silent as to the issue of 'privacy,' that term not appearing there or anywhere else in the Constitution, the *Roe* court decided it was there nevertheless as "emanating," "radiating," or existing within the "penumbra" of the Fourteenth Amendment, taken as a whole. That is, the very terms of the Fourteenth Amendment along with the Bill of Rights, *in toto*, themselves implicitly set forth a right of privacy upon which the state statute in question was found to intrude. These kinds of inventions along with other unsubstantiated assumptions offered by the Court have not, do not and will not well stand the test of time.

Thus, from the language of the Fourteenth Amendment the Court extracted "privacy" as being a matter of Constitutional law which provided the Court with jurisdiction and then proceeded to hold it protected abortion, painting here with a broad brush. Up to this time it was generally accepted that state law, or municipal law, or local law if you will, provided and was responsible for the protection of the safety, health, morals and welfare of the populus in accordance with the Tenth Amendment. *Roe* instead brought abortion into the federal ambit under a newly found Constitutional right of privacy. In other words, individual policy [abortion laws (laws frame policy)] was essentially legislated by the high Court after finding that the rights of liberty and notions of privacy are so deeply rooted in the conscience and traditions of the people as to be nothing other than "...ranked as fundamental [to the Constitution]."

In spite of what the public may have read or been told, at base what the *Dobbs* court did was to return this issue to the States while at the same time commenting [obiter dicta] that the

Constitution did not prohibit abortion, quite contrary to what the media said such as the Court had "outlawed abortion" or in effect held it to be unconstitutional [which is not true – and it didn't].

However it is viewed, the issue itself is not being dealt with here as either right or wrong but rather how the *Roe* opinion changed politics and politicking in the United States, and created a new specie of voter, the 'one issue voter' now added alongside the exclusive party line voter.

The ferocious national fracture and split this single case created has also not served the country well causing some voters to not take other more critical issues into their decisional equations which sorely deserve independent attention, that is, ignoring other issues of greater consequence to the nation as a whole. On this point, few if any would disagree, without casting aspersions of any kind with reference to which side of the issue one may find themselves.

While *Dobbs* has returned the issue to the people and their elected state representatives per the Tenth Amendment, and although this will not end the melee, it does put the matter closer to the will of the voters at the state level of government. Regardless of what one may say or think, medical science will render the entire matter moot in the near future. People will then look back on the entire epochal matter as a wholly avoidable, ghastly social tearing, the Court having stepped into a legislative quagmire of its own making on a par with its many rulings with reference to the 'peculiar institution*.' Worse, it has visited upon not just men and women, but women among themselves the highest case of irreconcilable differences and divisiveness.

This brief jurisprudential review of these two abortion opinions sets the stage for examining the pending *Relentless* case which will both directly and indirectly affect the personal lives of all Americans.

Relentless, Inc. v. Department of Commerce challenges the constitutional propriety of the Congress delegating to its legislatively created agencies [FTC, EPA, ICC, FCC, DHS, etc.] plenary and horizontally encompassing powers to regulate (legislate), enforce (executive action) and review (judicial like authority) matters coming before them. Upon an exhaustion of all administrative proceedings, only then could the matter in question even be reviewed by a court. Pursuant to the doctrine laid down in the *Chevron* case decided in 1984 [again, Chevron, U.S.A., Inc. v. Natural Resources Defense Council, Inc., 467 U. S. 837] it was held that a reviewing court must defer to an agency's reasonable interpretations of statutes and administrative rulings, and to rely upon and adopt the 'expert' findings of such agencies supposedly operated by appointees trained and experienced in the area of expertise with which they may be dealing.

On the face of the matter the *Chevron* court mandated 'leaving what the experts say in place if reasonable' as courts are not necessarily trained or experienced in such special matters may facially seem fair and appropriate. However, what Congress has done, it is challenged in *Relentless*, is to have delegated away its own constitutional legislative authority and responsibilities. Further, it has also delegated to the agency in question the powers of both the judicial and executive branches of government. This, it is argued, violates the separation of powers doctrine, a fundamental principle of the U. S. Government.

*

The *Roe* Court decided in a split decision that access to abortion was a 'good thing' and permissible as a matter of federal law [a legislative call] and found the statute being tested before it too restrictive and/or unequally applicable in accessing such services. It then 'legislated' several guidelines to go along with its underlying holding.

This intrusion by a handful of lawyers appointed to the Court into the private lives of citizens has lit up the political sky with fireworks [to put it in the most charitable of terms] ever since. From the political and social stand points the nation's future was recast. In so doing the Court did the country no favors. Had it stayed within its constitutional role, decided what needed to be decided, and sent the case back to Texas [the court below], much suffering and damage could have been avoided. Whether the Court intended this, or foresaw this, or simply did not care will forever be debated. What is undeniable is the Court did make a federal foray into the private lives of the citizens, a matter seemingly left to the States or to the people in accordance with the Tenth Amendment. Ultimately, the *Dobbs* Court saw it that way as did the founders.

The *Roe* Court nevertheless decided to proceed to legislate and in so doing has again demonstrated an abject vacua of perspicacity and sagacity with reference to the effect its opinion would have on the nation, a point not overlooked by that court's own dissenting Justices.

Dobbs sent the abortion issue back to whence it came by returning the issue to the States. *Relentless* seeks to have government returned to Congress. There is an important parallel between *Dobbs* and *Relentless*, hence their inclusion here as both are basic constitutional matters along with the somewhat awkward posture of the Supreme Court having to reverse itself.

*

Some forty years ago the *Chevron* court trod a common path with *Roe*, to wit: It was a 'good thing.' In *Chevron* it was argued letting agencies carry out all three branches of government was a good thing and that their results should be deferred to by the courts if reasonable. Afterall, they are the experts. But what is left out of this mantra is that those who attempt to promote plenary powers for congressionally created agencies are actually pushing for the 'Administrative State,' a concept advanced by the politically oriented who seek to promote an ultimately totalitarian or very powerful and unaccountable central government in all matters. Regardless, the *Chevron* court agreed this was a good thing, and that was enough, and deference to agencies became the law.

*

Keep in mind that the term, 'Administrative State' (softball words crafted in an attempt to eliminate the true sting of the form of government it actually represents) is political speak by those interested in pressing socialism or a Marxist theory of government on the American people. It is this political attack which is the source of the present divisive political split in the nation and could well be the catalyst for much Jeffersonian blood.

Also keep in mind that the two camps are populated by those who favor the socio-Marxist form of government on the one hand, and the free enterprise representative form of government on the other, both now being deeply entrenched. For whatever reason or reasons, there now exists among the socio-Marxists members from the upper middle class and the elites, and considerable numbers from the working and non-working class those who call themselves 'Progressives.' It is curious they refer to themselves as Progressives while wanting to take the country back to what it experienced which our forebearers fought so hard to escape, to wit: a heavy-handed centralized form of government led by one person (or a few persons) with power, a leader with indeed unimaginable powers. Therefore, they might more accurately be named Regressives, not Progressives. While claiming they want to progress to something 'new' and presumably better, it is given a politically pleasing but misleading moniker, a not uncommon practice and political ploy. Whatever the case, it is a choice the American citizens will have to decide with their votes.

At the same time there are some at the lower levels of society who are perfectly willing to give up their freedoms to those ranking above them for security in return which would ultimately in the final analysis represent ninety-five percent or more of the population, the others holding party rank with privileges along with the professionals. There are elites who are more than happy to take over the power structures and managerial functions of a socio-Marxist architecture of governmental control to carry out policy handed down by the national leadership. Both camps think they are right. Again, it is *this* which is the underlying basis of the divisiveness and present bitter political clash in the nation. Each side has its arguments. As to this point, this is a free nation, and the choice is up to the citizens. One is free to vote oneself into a socialistic or Marxist form of government, but there will be challenges to get out of it, and it will not entail voting.

*

The rub in the congressionally created agency structure described, *supra*, is what might be a 'good thing' is not necessarily constitutional. Good or not, whether pervasive and extensive congressional delegation of authority to agencies is constitutional or not is back before the Court in *Relentless*. In other words, *Relentless* is going to be a constitutional replay and review of *Chevron* as *Dobbs* was for *Roe*.

The Constitutional question brought into focus here is whether Congress can create agencies which write the rules, test the rules for compliance deciding whether or not someone has violated such rules, and then enforce them with fines, lockdowns, or whatever measures are decided upon? Again, Congress has delegated not just its own authority to the agencies it created, but also vested in them powers testing compliance [a judicial function] and powers of enforcement [an executive function]. Or, from the legal perspective, does this over-arching new architecture of agencies run afoul of the separation of powers doctrine clearly delineated in the separate Articles I, II and III of the Constitution?

Observe that agencies are of great convenience to Congress as the issues and authority delegated to them take such matters out of its hands, off its docket, and gives it insulation from public reaction. Being a member of Congress now moves even closer to Utopia so far as its members and workload are concerned, having already taken care of their remunerative benefits and opportunities of all kinds, present and future.

As the Court put abortion issues back into the hands of the several States, it will now decide if congressional responsibilities need be put back into the hands of Congress along with judicial and executive activities being returned to their respective branches. Do the rules which not just affect but govern the lives of citizens have to be in the hands of their elected officials who are answerable, or may such powers be delegated to unelected appointees who are not? There are several styles of government where officials are not answerable to the people. *That* is what is at stake. And *this* is of importance as agencies do indeed affect the lives of the citizens in profound ways, hence its serious importance to individuals.

The Court is faced with a daunting task. The complexities are not just myriad, but laden with unknowns as was the case in *Roe*. Unforeseen, nigh unforeseeable consequences will spawn a parade of second-guessers. Depending on what the Court does, it may have to re-visit the issue and refine its opinions several times. Yet, sympathy is difficult to muster as in both *Roe* and *Chevron* the Court did it to itself, put itself into its own political nightmare. Had the High Court in *Chevron* simply adhered to constitutional principles the issue before it would not have ended up back in the Court and much of its integrity [its only asset] preserved, separation of powers being a generally recognized and understood constitutional construct.

*

The Chief Justice has observed, "Our role is very clear. We are to interpret the Constitution and the laws of the United States and insure the political branches act within them." This and issues of law [judicial review] are its sole responsibility. To go beyond it is dicta ['commentary,' not law], and any feint at or outright legislation is absolutely without authority, but sometimes the Court does so anyway. Therefore, how can the high Court expect other branches of government to not exercise extra-legal activities when it does so itself? When it does so itself, how can it legitimately or even practically expect its own orders to be carried out? It can't. The fact is the government has failed to observe the rule of law. All truth is spoken through behavior. Net result..., ultimately a failed state if we are not careful.

*

Make no mistake, the Supreme Court has been an excellent court with some excellent Justices. It has been a cohesive body relatively free of petulant querulousness. It has usually enjoyed a commonality of opinion with 9-0 opinions having been the most common vote alignment. When it legislates, not so much. Currently it is struggling.

Keep an eye on the Court. What it does affects you. It affects your daily lives. There are those who want to force it to do what Congress does not want to do or refuses to do. There be demons in this tension.

Why not become a Lawyer, Pilgrim?

YOUR COUNTRY:

IV

EDUCATION

Consider fundamental basic education, the kind which develops the mind, teaching it to think, providing it with abilities and techniques which later can be generalized to other problem-solving settings, and the ability to generate solutions to life's challenges and difficulties, the sort of public education which was required as the nation was developing.

Where is the inculcation of an understanding and respect for a free country and its form of government, the price for which had to be paid with rivers of men's blood to bring it to life, with more floods to protect it, and the responsibility of all to protect and preserve it if we wish to remain free and enjoy its benefits? Read the Declaration of Independence* and the histories of the men who signed it. It is all online.

*

Most of the nation's youth cannot add [they cannot carry], let alone subtract ['borrowing' a number from the adjacent column of the minuend (just a one {1})] is beyond their uneducated comprehension [they were never taught to think abstractly]. Forget about multiplication, division or the calculation or derivation of a root and the magic of exponents. Important and serious? Yes, if they are ever able to have the ability to understand and comprehend basic economics, tax policy, and spending both personally and from the public fisc. Today, most are only interested in and will listen to what politicians say they will give them. Prisoners of promises, shibboleths and false hopes. Glittering generalities. And you are *their* prisoners as they will vote for their own politicized personal interests based on what they have been told and not those of the nation. I refer to them as 'they' because they will not be reading this as you are for reasons unique to you and unnecessary to pitch here.

He who controls the children will control the nation.

To get an idea of what's going on here, take a look at an 'eighth-grade public school final examination*' from one hundred years ago (that is approximately three generations --- likely your grandparents or great grandparents took it). There are several, go ahead. It's on the web <Eighth-Grade Final Exam>. You will quickly get the idea. Why all of those 'difficult' subjects; Math, physics, civics, literature, languages, geography and its many influences, history, logic, the arts, even Latin, Greek culture with a dollop of the ancient Romans, if you really want to drill down? To what possible use could such subjects ever be put? The modern educator must not think much of them anymore. Curriculums have been gutted. Or maybe there simply are not the necessary teachers who can manage or are permitted to manage what is challenging and developmental, both intellectually and civically? Or maybe the political card has been played and they have been eliminated from the curricula to make for gullible voters.

The 'teachers' are often [far from always] lame, robotic script followers who enjoy a reliable paycheck and summers off. Then perhaps it is of their own doing. Their dependency on the system has kept their salaries below, usually, that of lawyers, doctors and engineers. However, the good ones choose to teach anyway because that is what they love. They know they can make a difference. Or, put differently, because they love it, they are good. Too many are not nowadays, of course you already know that.

Maybe policy considerations of educating the public have changed, or is it that administrators simply see or are forced to see 'relevant' curricula differently from the past in this new world. Have politics or preferences actually found their way into public education? It *has* changed.

Civics has not just disappeared, it has fallen into disfavor. Few are even able to conceptualize the subject. I wonder why that has happened? Perhaps it would be better to call it public indoctrination? Why is that? Does indifferent, careless, irresponsible behavior coupled with quiescence and the inability or lack of motivation to intelligently object inexorably flow from prosperity? Or maybe it is governmental paternalism, or politicians whose priorities are in seeking their own benefits rather than those of the citizens they represent? Stupid or ignorant voters are easier to convince. Politicians themselves may even now be the product of the new order. Listen to them critically. Observe their behavior. Perhaps something else? You might discuss this with your parents and grandparents. You will be surprised about how much they know.

They are apt to point out that among the haves, now becoming a distinct minority, want control and a permanent position in a two-tiered social hierarchy where the have nots [95%+ in the final new order] only want security at any cost. Then if both sides get what they want it is supposed, at least according to political theory, quiescence will reign. After all, it has been the most prolific architecture of governments over the entire course of the political history of the earth, and indeed still is. The number of people living under this regime far outnumber those who do not. But this is not the purpose behind the founding of this free nation.

Freedom has been thought to be the natural and inalienable right of mankind with governmental powers deriving from the consent of the governed.

Public education, if it is to be education at all, must provide more than just selective information. It should develop the mind so as to be able to think abstractly, to anticipate and recognize problems, to be able to proceed through a regime of testability, and process constructs* through one's own mental equations and formulas of conceptual or formal thought, whether it is acquired in accordance with the Ausubelian school or the Brunerian school, or based on any other theory of learning for that matter. Even Vygotsky is fine, a defensible learning theory. It makes little difference, ultimately. The ends and abstract abilities are ultimately much the same, the ability of oneself to think for oneself. It has to be built into the youngsters along their developmental journey. Virtually all of them can get it. Anything less isn't education. I'm not sure today's fare rises to the level of useable information or even training. Simply put, education's prime mission should be to inculcate the ability to think and solve problems. Education is what is left after the factual materials have been pretty much forgotten.

Education today seems to be more of a string of information bits selected by governments' bureaucracies, along with 'standards' for testing (This must be taught, that must not be..., and the corresponding tests passed, which in some locales most students, if not all, do not). It typically does not even rise to the level of even the most basic of training. It doesn't teach how to think, it teaches what to think. Recognizing laudable exceptions, public education does not even teach how to do something, anything.

Do not fool yourselves, a national disaster is in the making. A national disaster is in the making, and it has been underway for more than a generation. While the majority simply do not see it, or ignore it, there is now national change in the air. Ill-equipped cohorts are moving into power.

Get yourself ready. And along with this, an uninformed or misinformed public will destroy the purpose of democratically elected representatives forming a republic. Demagogues are recasting the nation by propagandizing too many helpless, hapless voters who simply do not understand government.

There may be a solution. Of course. Bigger schools, smaller classes, more money for the teachers, and double the size and pay of the administration to get the 'very best' while adding lots of new diversified courses, something which might lead to a job. Possibly teaching 'how' to do something is the answer. That makes sense. Parents will buy it if they are around. This will lead to a job that pays something and gets the kids out of the basement. The student's education is now seemingly valuable to him or her, and it is also now of value to the state.

If this new approach to regulated education (matching training with the job markets) becomes too expensive, eliminate the arts (both performing and aesthetic) and athletics, of course [read competitive sports]. Eliminate the intellectual subjects; philosophy, civics, history, metaphysics, composition, Latin, The Golden Age of nations and their fall. What do they have to do with our culture, our national integrity, our ability to fulfill our civic responsibility as citizens and voters? Isn't it the jobs, stupid?! Isn't it? That's what you read. Or are jobs (training) and education mutually exclusive while still standing on some balance of equal footing?

Anyway, why bother? It is now all hand holding anyway. Every kid gets a trophy. Just show up. Whose idea was that? Maybe the nation is now truly fueled by hope and promises for change, or has it been fooled into downfall? Is it anywhere now taught that the price of gaining and preserving freedom along with the resultant benefits of opportunity are high, and they can be easily lost? Is it anywhere now taught that discipline, commitment, and restraint are required for success, for the nation's preservation? Is it anywhere now taught, no matter what one's job may be, that doing it well contributes to the nation's success as well as one's own? Should it be said that anyone doing their job well is a responsible citizen and should be recognized as such? Does government management of the employed and the unemployed [both a politically created class] make for a functioning constitutional republic and a strong nation? Do not forget, a good education is based in the home.

*

What about the value and importance of educated voters having a basic sense of economics and history, of civics and political responsibility, of the value of family, community, and commitment? Are they not among the social pillars of a free, secure, and democratic society? Do most students today know what it takes to succeed? Do they even know what success is? Do they even care? Are new order freedoms to be found in pornography, abortion, no-fault, lack of restraint and falsehoods; politics by shibboleth, advertisement, monikers and sparkling mantras driven by the networks as they extoll the virtues of those up for election with whom they have aligned? They offer up alluring messages seeking to attract the support of the most vulnerable, helpless, and uninformed among us to whom later are given a handout.

*

How could any group or anyone with even a crumb of integrity and honesty engender such dependence? What has brought the nation here? What has happened to the underlying foundations of integrity, independence, respect, truth, responsibility, universally accepted and time-honored standards of morality, simple decency, and why?

Are you able to imagine where the nation would be today if its people were disciplined, the social order well-structured and loyally supportive, with all resources fully developed, along with productive citizens and businesses fostered without interference, governmental influence or obstruction? Are you able to imagine where the nation would be today if politicians put the interests of the people they represent ahead of their own? Are you? Give it some thought.

The message to you? Your education; make the most of it. For nearly everyone, it only comes around once.

Why not become a teacher, Pilgrim?

V
ECONOMICS

Do Americans not have even the foggiest idea let alone the wisp of any concern as to what wealth is all about? What is required for a nation to successfully interact among nations? This is supposed be a nation of free enterprise. What is it that permits such a nation to economically thrive and flourish? Upon what are its strengths based? Are the fundamentals generally known? Is it even taught?

Basic economics, the underlying financial support systems and its management, are profoundly simple. All important principles are profoundly simple. Name one that isn't. It is politics which foster confusion compounded by the politically compliant 'economists.' Interest groups then further poison the well.

Economists, for whom the truly educated have little regard, say it is complex. It isn't. Perhaps after they have added their arcane babble and varied political tilts it becomes confusing. By developing a recondite language and making selective social assumptions they have succeeded in creating an 'intellectual' club. They refer to it as a discipline. It isn't and it isn't. This 'science' is undisciplined, polarized, inconsistent, and loaded with false assumptions to foster a result. It is typically useless as a reliable business or governmental planning device in a free enterprise system. Science it is not.

To make matters worse, it has fractured itself into political allegiances, some supporting the 'administrative state*,' some promoting the fruits of 'free enterprise*' while some now even being essentially anti-American in opposition to its founding principles, to name a few. Top-down accountability finds no place in any discussion of democratic principles, a plan which is not only false, but a constitutional fraud. That is not the architecture of this Republic. The government as designed is accountable to the citizens. A Democratic Republic is *not* built on top-down control while most other governments are. Again, read the Constitution.

Typical of economists and academics [and often appellate judges], they make false assumptions [or assumptions which allow them to proceed to a predestined conclusion] and then buildup on them with exhausting, irrelevant rationalizations to the point where the reader has forgotten that upon which the argument was made in the first place. With this approach the various worlds of economists operate under a variety of different colors. Some are influenced by precepts of free enterprise. Others by socialism. Some are influenced or guided by fascism, collectivistic or communistic theories. Some go for globalism. Others, profit or control at any cost. Thus, they cannot claim to be a science when they disagree more than they agree, and that their positions arise from the fact they are now in reality only political tools. Not all, but enough emerge to make it look like a club of fools who don't get along.

At base, a nation has two and only two sources of wealth: useful natural resources and productive human resources (labor combined with knowledge) fairly compensated to participate in production, the *externalities* of economics. As a fundamental matter, nothing else. Everything is built from there up. From this, all economics flow.

Economic success comes down to these two basic foundations of origin. This paradigm is the Primary [or First] Financial Principle of Economics. The Secondary [or Second] Financial Principle works at the peripheries, the machinery or *internalities* of the economic engine discussed *infra*. Without access to at least one of these foundational resources [human or naturally occurring], a nation in a world economy cannot successfully participate let alone compete. Mere traders have never done very well and have little if any geopolitical influence or leverage. They may be able to make deals skimming as they go, it may be precariously sustained by gray markets, but as with all middlemen, they ultimately wither on the vine of the stream of commerce the moment a better efficiency appears. Both resources, I suppose, may be imported, or dealt with on a business basis from abroad, but the system is precarious and vulnerable. The nation which thrives in the long run has both, domestically.

Then there are nations which have one and import or export the other, but take note, they are unstable, and at the mercy of logistics and well-endowed neighbors. A nation without either, I suppose, is effectively relegated to an economic system where people 'sell insurance to one another.'

Economists will go into apoplexy over this as it is 'too simple,' but it is the truth. However, this is what the U.S. has been doing to one degree or another over the past several years and putting it on your tab [hot checks coupled with deficit monetary politics (votes and inside financial opportunities) perhaps creating the illusion of prosperity but in reality putting the nation's inflation on steroids]. In so doing, the U. S. government is taking the nation down an unsustainable economic/financial path by profligate spending and printing of money thereby adding to the national debt at a rate faster than the growth of the Gross National Product (the total value of goods and services produced by the entire nation), saddling the nation with the invisible tax of inflation which has also been not only outrunning the GNP but winning an international race to the economic graveyard. The politicians [your representatives] have even managed to create a deficit that now *exceeds* the annual GNP. If you look closely at where that deficit money is going, your 'money,' you will observe it is being spent for votes or 'friends' abroad. In the long-run, peace and national friendship cannot be bought. Again, your money, your debt. Agree or disagree, any fair-minded assessment would be challenged to conclude otherwise.

*

The inherent wealth of natural resources is operationally self-defining. When resources are used by humans who are engaged in the intellectual and physical production of something of greater value than the material with which they started, and placed into the *stream of commerce*, commercial wealth is then created commensurate with the Primary Financial Principle. All other participants, no matter what they do or how they contribute, are along for the ride and soak up whatever portion of that wealth which may come their way as profits, fees, commissions or "pay" in the chain and process of, *inter alia*, planning, management and delivery consistent with and constituting the Secondary Financial Principle [Tertiary being waste (including excessive Secondary costs), crime, irresponsible government and general mismanagement]. Thus, the Secondary Financial Principle relates to non-productive services associated with the legitimate streams of commercial activities which are undeniably necessary to make the economic engine run, a *sine qua non* of the end result. However, they in fact take from the fundamental wealth produced and therefore share in the fruits of its creation and the revenues ultimately generated.

Included in this phase of the economic engine are necessary administrative, marketing, logistical and supportive participants not directly productive in nature, their value being measured against a standard of highest efficiency and market competition. Also taken from the First Financial Principle of production are, *inter alia*, profits to the owners and equity holders, returns on investment and speculators' bounty, that is, those who put at risk the needed venture capital to start, build and develop economic engines.

Again, 'economists' would like to hold it to be far more complicated than this. It isn't so far as fundamental wealth is concerned. Fundamental wealth is the combining of resources and labor. From there the economic strata starts and is accordingly diluted with the economic service side simply superimposed. Knowledge and efficiency then become the challenge played out in the crucible, as it were, of competition associated with intellectual activity and free market practices. Any economy which stands on other than this basic wealth stratagem has feet of clay, is artificially manipulated and strategically vulnerable. Whether this would survive the scrutiny of a dissertation committee as being devoid of the expected bovine scatology is bovine scatology.

This economic terminology and the principles which it represents may be unfamiliar, but their elegance and power arise from clarity, simplicity, understandability and universal applicability. Its usefulness and the principles displayed are relevant to not just businesses alone, but nations, even the world at large. They are as immutable as the revelation of the last universal economic paradigm, the relationship between supply and demand, also elegant in its simplicity and powerful in its universality. Addressing the economics of, *inter alia*, management, markets, taxes, trade policies, etc., is beyond the scope of the basic foundation message here.

Look around the world. It is all rather obvious. Wealthy nations either have resources or acquire resources and apply the effects of labor to them. The most successful have both, and husband both as a matter of national policy. Some countries provide raw materials to other counties where cheap labor (destituting in accordance with U. S. standards) or slavish labor is added, the resulting products then being competitively introduced into the stream of commerce with towering profits made off the backs of others while keeping the market locked. Here, those in control of labor do well; the workers themselves everywhere, not so much. Merchandizers at the end of the chain rake in their profits from the sale of relatively cheap goods. The university business schools say this is good. Can you imagine that? Do you wonder why? Is this not the hoped-for result from the architecture, mechanics and fundamental underpinnings of socialism? Is it, or isn't it? Make big promises to the little guy, then strangle his contribution out of him.

A value judgment is not being called for here, but it seems fair to say it presents an issue worthy of your thought. At some point you will have to choose. Or perhaps better put, it will be chosen for you, if you get my drift.

One might wonder if some court somewhere, say SCOTUS, would find a state statute [or federal, which I doubt would ever see the light of day given congressional international entanglements] which prohibited introduction into a state's stream of commerce goods manufactured by slave, prisoner or unfairly underpaid paid workers constitutional? Just asking. Voters are constantly hearing about all the integrity and fair dealing of the new candidates running for office who are pledging to end corruption in Washington, promising to create and protect 'good paying' jobs for all the workers, and to bring morality back to government, each one pledging to make the nation once again a respected global member.

*

A few countries are well endowed with resources and simply market them to the world, and because they participate in this specialized stream of commerce their governments pretty much take care of its citizens and all their needs (often with America's unneeded assistance but given for political reasons - called foreign aid - another soft-ball moniker - actually politics being played on an international stage). This makes for some, shall we say, complicated geo-politics particularly in view of potential interruptions of the supply, pricing or distribution choices of their commodities. Think oil-rich nations next door to a modern-day population of Huns*.

One might reasonably conclude that the United States now has a policy of refusing to develop natural resources as well as the necessary human factors (read, *inter alia*, jobs and an educated and trained populace to perform them), demonetizing both. Clearly it husbands neither. It tightly controls both for political reasons including engendered dependency. Comprehensible given the leadership, but completely incomprehensible given the needs of the nation, the purpose of free enterprise, its national security, and the constitutional oath taken by every office holder. Behold the nation's energy resources. Strangled. The resource of energy and the independence it fosters is more vital to your safety, economic security, and stability than your government would like to have you believe, the very safety of your streets and neighborhoods.

Bureaucracies and administrators are among the biggest soakers, with their numbers and inefficiencies being difficult to rein in as they seem to self-procreate in the process of working to justify their existence and increase their numbers. Insurance, taxes, packaging, transportation, transmission, etc., and the list is long, are all important, all necessary within practical and efficient limits for a successful economic machine. In excess, [Tertiary Financial Principles; graft, and crime aside] they unnecessarily subtract from fundamental wealth and the health of the economy, weakening competitive strength. No worries economists content, it is not all bad. They get paid and spend, and are therefore 'productive.' Without them we would have a lesser economy. Any time money moves is a good thing. That is how economists think. But it is the free economy, the free enterprise system which culls those who are, let us say in polite terms, inefficient. Fundamentally, true wealth is the capital of resources and labor in combination; in other words, the efficient productive use and integration of investment with both labor and material driven by free enterprise exercised in open commerce. The law is capable of dealing with abuses.

If productivity is stifled, resources artificially limited, or labor is not efficient or incapable, fundamental wealth is compromised. The system begins to weaken into a downward spiral with an upward spiral of 'social' spending, and inflation emerges along with other avoidable deficit spending with any recovery coming at a very high cost if ever at all, and in more ways than economic. Or, operationally put, trading cheap labor in another country for poverty at home is an equation for disaster. This is violative of the trust of office in a republic. This breach could well be followed by the unthinkable specter of a class revolt [particularly giving the emerging social and societal issues, and nascent mindlessly entrenched political positions now being taken noted *supra*]. This is your nation, Pilgrim.

A job is more than an economic event. Work feeds the psyche and the social side of life as much as it does the wallet. We identify with and take pride in what we do. We are what we do. You have observed the result of taking it away. Perhaps your life has been cast because of it. Remember, each individual success benefits all of us as each failure burdens all.

Outsourcing jobs may have a profit incentive for businesses, but for whom and at what cost to others? When the government fostered international trade agreements seeking 'cheap' goods during the past decades, what did it have in mind? To whom did the monetary benefits flow? Were there special relationships between a chosen few in this land with governments, businesses and leaders in foreign lands? Is that lawful or in accordance with the rule of law or its intent? Perhaps the plan was to also generate more poor folks here who are now dependent or partially yet necessarily dependent on those in government who impoverished them in the first place along with ubiquitous assurances of wide-ranging public services, safety nets and support systems..., and votes? Hope fiercely?

This is something which is easy to research. All anyone needs to do is simply observe for themselves if they can strip blind 'loyalties' out of their thinking and politics. Make your own judgments while remembering all truth is spoken through behavior. The citizens and their representatives better get their politics right if they want America to survive as a free, strong, safe and prosperous nation.

Added to this is the problem of promises to continually pay additional recipients increasing streams of money to people no longer in the workforce, or about to leave it, or were never in it in the first place, with other benefits attached from the public fisc, and it is staggering. If the economy is 'permitted' to flag, or tanked by politicians, problems will worsen by putting recessionary trends into inflation's spin cycle. They compound one another. As with deficit spending and inflation, or the over-regulation of the economy into ultimate collapse, they are all inseparable. The politicians' response, 'it's necessary as there is an unmet public need.' But it is the least among us who simply do not understand and who will be hurt the most as they vote for shibboleths and catch-words. Kill free enterprise and you kill the kind of prosperous economy it can create. To politicize economics is to poison the economy.

The economists' arcane political response: 'homeostatic-like forces will eventually bring equipoise,' and they get paid for saying it. Fools. That which is artificially controlled or manipulated for the benefit of some rather than the whole nation is not homeostatic, nor is it free enterprise.

*

It ought to be well-nigh obvious that profligate political spending cannot continue. It cannot be practiced *ad infinitum* without leading to economic failure. Revolution as the by-product has historically been witnessed and is again being witnessed around the world. Take a look. You have no idea what you could be in for as you have experienced only a modicum of peace and prosperity. Foreign armies have not yet come to your shores, your neighborhoods. Armed residents have not yet turned on one another. With regard to what war will be like for you is not what you see in the media or in theaters. It has been filtered, censored. The truth is unimaginable.

Many Americans do not see this, or they do not want to look, or maybe they don't even care, or perhaps a different sociological pathology is at work? Maybe repression? Suppression? Were they kept blind and stupid by selfish politicians, all enhanced by the media [under educated, inexperienced, unaccomplished ne'er-do-wells who sit on the sidelines of life and whine while blindly carrying their assigned banners]?

And what happens when the income tax combined with all the other taxes compounded by inflation reaches a point where taxpayers will tolerate economic oppression no more? Will they tolerate an *ad valorem* tax where one is effectively being forced to buy (or pay for) the same property again and again? At the same time property values themselves, including appreciated values are soaked up via dilution of the dollar by government paying over to people who never did, do not, or never will make a contribution to the nation's treasury, or even the peripheral wealth or shadow economy, let alone pay any income taxes or in any way contribute to the public fisc. If the government lets the national debt continue to run wild, taxing unrealized gains on appreciated assets and investments is next.

The government is not a business let alone run like a business, and if it were to participate in the creation of fundamental wealth it would, true to form, be irresponsible, wasteful and corrupt. And when tax upon tax seems to be reaching its tolerable end, might not government just print more money? This is what your government does. Look at its history. Even though this is in reality a tax, few notice it. It may look like a gift, but actually it is an insidious economic disease. Writing hot checks to capture a voting base and pay interest on the national debt will ultimately lead to failure. It is on the way to destroying your country.

It *is* happening Pilgrim, now, and it is accelerating.

*

Is deficit spending not a "taking" constitutionally speaking? Is there not something in the Constitution about the public taking of private property without compensation? Isn't deflating the value of one's wealth by government fiat a taking? Is that lawful or within the drafters' plan? Are there not at least some constitutional limits? Note and think about the last clause of the Fifth Amendment, the 'Famous Fifth,' laden with as of yet unthought-of implications. Think about it.

Why not just an out and out grab of private assets, cash accounts which are 'deemed' to be 'overly' exorbitant, unnecessary, unfair, inequitable, to fund the government? Why not land? A home where several families could be put up. Never happened, right? Russia, Germany, China, Cuba, Venezuela, etc.? Even Italy took a second look. France peeked. Who knows what governments will do when their existence becomes threatened?

*

We have heard that government recklessly taxes and spends. Actually, it is the other way around; the government recklessly spends (attendant to political and financial interests – also read votes and personal gain), and then taxes (or prints money electronically or in currency simply ignoring a soaring deficit which you or your blood will eventually have to pay). Taxes are either directly levied or the value of the dollar is reduced via deficit spending. Both are taxes. Recklessness doesn't adequately define it. Carelessness doesn't adequately define it. It is something else, isn't it?

The upshot is the same; the government spending money it does not have casting debt upon you. Is the debt this creates "lawful" within the meaning of the Constitution? It seems some creative lawyer ought to be able to come up with a constitutional theory, an argument. Would the High Court find this effrontery as being political and not being within its jurisdiction? At the same time, are not officials sworn to uphold the Constitution and protect the nation [read the citizens] from enemies, both foreign *and* domestic? Might not the High Court stretch far enough to recognize that which the drafters intended encompasses this issue? It has 'stretched' before.

This is just something to think about as novel constitutional issues are surely to be presented to the High Court in the future as frequently as they have been in the past. Yet the High Court has been heard to say, 'we don't get involved in politics or political activities.' Really? That would bring on an international guffaw. Nevertheless, whatever that Court might do is apt to be better than what congress has done, will do, has failed or refused to do.

What is the salient significance of the existing economic status of the United States, and why is it mentioned here? The country is in a pre-war setting. Do not delude yourself. Do not let the media delude you. It is here. Profligate deficit spending has weakened the nation. The nation is vulnerable. Vulnerability invites attack. As the United States finds itself engulfed in more and more multiple global conflicts, and then outright world war, whirlwind deficit spending will soar to unmanageable heights beyond anything witnessed presently. Whatever money you have, if you can get to it, will become nearly worthless. Most in government know this [while some, pathetically, do not]. Ask your Congressman. Yet the government continues to wildly spend before the first strikes against us have even been launched. If they are directed against the United States homeland, and there is no reason to think that they will not be, the nation's ability to respond will be crippled.

When will this occur? Any time, now through to the end of the decade. Military men will tell you it will be closer to the former than the latter. There will be no 'arsenal of democracy,' there will be no 'Manhattan Project,' as there will be no time. It will, for practical purposes, be over essentially *instanter*.

Message? Start by getting your politics right, be guided by the interests of the nation. If you don't get your politics right, there will be no politics to get right. Maybe get a license to take matters into the courts and get the national economics straightened out. Bring to the courts those matters with which Congress refuses to deal. Is there any other way? It has been done before.

Why not run for office, Pilgrim?

VI

CRIME

In the world of crime, where to start? It is evolving faster than this manuscript can be updated. The face of crime, where it is being committed, why, how, by whom, its effects and consequences are changing, insidiously mutating into generalized lawlessness. Cause, data, societal reaction, borders, political response, its own micro economies both before and after the fact, there seems to be no end. Maybe start with the fact that even before recent events, the United States has been the most imprisoned culture(s) and country on earth. In fact, there are sub-groups within the society where over half of its members are convicted felons (not just felons by deed), or have been incarcerated, are presently serving sentences, many more than once, or are otherwise having been or are 'in the system.' Added to this is the fact most criminals are not even apprehended in the first place. If they are, most are released without any meaningful controls. Most reported crimes are not solved. Most crimes are not even reported (read as one in ten in some quarters, or fewer). Today there are 'leaders' who simply ignore even the most public and violent of crimes. "It's not their fault, they are not to blame. It is society's fault." "It's free speech!" "They had no opportunity." "It is only a demonstration." Why is that, Pilgrim?

Crime must be a viable alternative lifestyle, it must pay, or perhaps there are no other alternatives. It is a way to make a living coming with paid vacations and a guaranteed retirement if things don't work out. Difficult to imagine, is it not? Totally incomprehensible you say, as incomprehensible as 9/11, simply not being within the bank of reason let alone possibilities. But it is happening, more is coming, and the upward curve will not just continue, but accelerate. Do not delude yourself, we are devolving into an uncivil war in our cities, then towns and then neighborhoods. Again, who is it that swore to uphold the Constitution (which is the United States) against all enemies, foreign and domestic? Everyone who holds public office. What is it that has destroyed the fundamental structures of the culture, its pillars, the glue of a society and nation, its ethics, its values, its ethos, its morals, the very spirit which holds it together? Well, Pilgrim, what is it?

*

Crime costs the nation more than education, and it is exploding. Both are simply different forms of waste of our own making [consistent with the Tertiary Financial Principle, see: *supra*]. Most people do not like crime, most like education and perennially more money is spent on both with perennially less to show for it. That is interesting. There must be something else, some other variable than money at work undermining one of the nation's foundations. Uneducated youth, an emerging criminal culture, or is it something deeper than that?

Both groups, the convicted and the uneducated, suffer in the realm of employability and can't perform up to any acceptable par even on standardized tests developed to create the illusion of success, "...tailored to be relevant, fair, sensitive to their needs and feelings, and respectful to those in today's world." But wait, obesity and its many clinical sequela may be the winners in the race to the deficit pit. It will be close. Just think, a "transformed America" populated by felons, ignoramuses, and the morbidly obese. Sorry, but so speaks the data.

The solution? Legalize gambling and THC along with its derivatives. Decriminalize crime. Give them cell phones. Dumb down school tests so they all pass. Send them checks. Simple enough. This will make lost souls happy. The new America, the transformed America, brimming with thoughts of hope and change, all a product of an intentionally stifled economy, a failing and politicized system of education, and keeping its citizens dependent and taking refuge in 'drugs,' now the leading killer of the young, [the leading killer *and* cause of long-term cognitive and psychic injuries] all based on "measures put in place." Sorry, but let us not be pessimistic as change will surely be visited upon the nation. It will, one way or another, without any need to hope for it. Maybe it is already here and just now being recognized.

Your thoughts, Pilgrim?

VII

DIVORCE

Divorce not that long ago was a criminal, or more commonly a quasi-criminal proceeding, and virtually unavailable to the crowd. Even the European aristocracy and later wealthy Americans had to resort to let us say other measures, extreme measures to obtain their desired relief. In Europe, it was wet work. In the U.S., it was a perverse use of mental health codes.

If there was a legally recognized right to a decree apart from mutual consent it was usually based on, *inter alia*, one of the parties criminal behavior of one sort or another, i.e., adultery, abuse, incarceration, abandonment, bringing an STD into the marriage, etc. To the parents or at least the grandparents of the reader of this book, the word divorce was unmentionable. Like abortion [Read 530 U. S. 914* to understand why], one couldn't use the term divorce, or the slur 'divorcee,' in polite company. Go ahead, ask your grandparents.

*

The most important decision one will make in his or her lifetime is who is chosen as a spouse. This choice is followed by with whom one associates which is followed by self or formal education [largely a function of reading] coupled with learning to do well whatever one does. All are the *sine qua non* of a successful life which itself is not dependent upon wealth. Do these things and money will come.

*

Today, prior to marriage, especially in cases where one or both of the parties to the planned wedding have substantial assets, have heritable expectancies, or are otherwise accustomed to seeking legal consultation in the ordinary course of their lives before doing anything legally or financially significant, seek a legal consult with an eye toward preplanning for divorce. This is not only common, but now advisable. Couples actually make preparations for divorce well before the marriage ever takes place, the now celebrated 'prenuptial agreement,' sometimes even confirmed in postnuptial agreements or contracts with titles to assets being adjusted voluntarily by conveyance, *antebellum*. Less often, new couples without significant assets, but who expect to later enjoy 'success' (in the Americanized sense) also anticipate and prepare for ending up in divorce court which commonly occurs because their hoped-for success actually comes to fruition. They now find themselves tripping over each other in their race to the 'family' court, or over others already there for no particularly good reason, or for reasons of their own making, or no responsible reason at all. How did that happen? The house of no-fault? Build it and they will come, the bonds of mutual effort and interdependency being vaporized.

In many circuit, commonwealth, parish, or state courts, divorce cases outnumber all other kinds of civil cases combined. In every jurisdiction, they exceed all other classes of civil cases. As a result, separate 'Divorce Courts' have even been set up to handle just matrimonial matters; the splitting of assets and the associated issues concerning the affected children, grandparents, or significant others, and the dog. They are now called 'Family Courts' to go along with Juvenile Courts, Drug Courts, and what not. Charming! The next court is left to your imagination, but it's coming. 'The guvmunt's gonna take care of it frum now on.' How did *that* happen?

By the time all factors are added up, more is lost in divorce courts, directly and indirectly, financially, emotionally, all with the permanent repercussions on children and future relationships in terms of trust, stability, their futures, deep-rooted traditions and the like, than from any other cause.

Several decades ago, state legislatures pursuant to vocal demands of a few passed what were dubbed 'no-fault divorce laws' where one party to a marriage could file a 'complaint' with a court and obtain a divorce typically only having to tell the judge, 'the objects of matrimony have been broken and there is no reasonable likelihood the marriage can be preserved' (or words to that effect) to which there is *no* defense. The other side cannot even argue that is not true [seeking to preserve the marriage]. A divorce decree will be entered. Many courts no longer even require such testimony on oath. Simply plead it in the complaint for divorce, or say it in open court on the record, or the lawyer may even say it for the client in some courts, and judgement will be entered. Or it can be accomplished by agreement, or upon the defendant's default in failing to file an answer or following the withdrawal of its answer to the suit. *Presto*! Divorced!

Generally, the court will require matters involving support, property and children to be resolved before the divorce is finalized, although there could be exceptions under 'exigent' circumstances. There are even cases where the court has entered judgment making its effective date at a point prior in time [known as *nunc pro tunc*, but of no significance here]. Nevertheless, the three-way contract of matrimony between the two partners of the marriage and the State can be broken at the will of one of the partners, and for no reason other than the testimony just quoted, true or not.

Half of marriages end in divorce, and the marriage failure rate for those who remarry is worse according to several studies, not surprisingly. The effect upon children is devastating, usually forever life scarring, the human glue of trust and family is forever destroyed, or at the very least shaken. It catapults through their lives forever changing structures of not only stability and trust in present relationships, but contaminates future relationships emotionally, by blood as well as by law, the failure of which is cast upon them tumbling on into following generations. There are exceptions, but few. [My, how much progress society has made.] Many never marry [So now we know where that 'phenomenon' comes from]. And the parents? Quite obviously they do not care and/or want to use proceedings as a weapon.

As a result, the family and all of that which is good, important, indeed critical flowing from it is disappearing. A sequela to all of this is that many, progressing to most, will simply never get married. Why even bother? Use your partner for so long as it is convenient.

*

During the mid twentieth century, illegitimacy rates were approaching five per cent and it was considered a national crisis, a catastrophe. Then it doubled in 1970. Today they are approaching fifty percent, and it's hardly discussed, indeed 'inappropriate' to even bring the subject up. It's insensitive. The rate is well over seventy-five percent in some settings. Some will say less, some will say more. 'Single mom' is now worn as a badge of respect. It even carries its own pronunciation moniker, 'single maum.' How remarkable the subtleties of language.

Telescoped out from the present trajectory, children will ultimately become wards [property] of the state. Nah! That can't be. That's never happened, has it? Anyway, it can't happen here, can it? Now tell me, what percent of the nation's children have already ended up in a governmentally operated 'family court' not to mention in schools directed and/or programed by government, or in the juvenile, drug and later criminal courts..., the 'justice system' as it were? Are there now High School clinics essentially serving as substitute parents providing drugs, contraceptives and gender counseling [how did they slip that by]? The answer is from fifty to approaching one hundred percent depending on what segment of society from which one is taking the sample. Splendid!

The 'social infrastructure' is already in place. For half of all children to again nearly one hundred percent in some settings, government run or programed schools [their agendas and services (clinics)] provide more sustenance, medical attention, 'guidance' and emotional support than do their parents. For many, the final result is the actual 'family' in effect becoming a failed institution [do you know where your kids are, do you know where your parents are, do you care?], the moral and ethical substructure of the family having been punted out of community's societal equation, yet this too is becoming an unmentionable in many settings as risking 'offending' others. What brought this about? What is it that is really occurring and why? Is this the face of the promised transformed America, some sort of liberation, or just the byproduct of the new legal philosophy of 'no-fault' gone awry? Something else? There is an answer.

*

Marry someone you know, not a recently met stranger. Marry someone who your parents know. Your chances for a successful marriage and long-term happiness will be exponentially enhanced.

Ask your parents and grandparents, Pilgrim.

VIII

MEDICAL SCIENCE

You live in a temple. That temple is not you. You are the one who resides there, a human being in residence. As with any residence, it needs attention, care and maintenance. Treat it well and it will treat you well. Occupy it with respect and honor and it will bring those same values to your existence. When that temple dies, it is returned to the earth. What previously resided there lives on. Therefore....

*

Medical technology today is a marvel; sensitive diagnostic equipment, computer assisted sweeping radiation beams forming biometric maps, minimally invasive endoscopic and laparoscopic surgical tools, CyberKnife therapies, targeted drugs, rehabilitative prosthetics, the emerging miracles of gene therapy, splitting and grafting, etc. The list is long. Much of this is beyond the imagination of practitioners even a single professional generation ago. But the treatment costs of this upward technological arc are as dramatic as the science itself, following, unfortunately, an even more accelerating geometric cost curve than that followed by the overall economy. Costs are on an exponential sprint.

So far as continuing research and costs going into even newer therapies and medicines, the same thing. Staggering, indeed, worse. The cost of research, testing, and development keeps some of the drug industry teetered on the financial brink. The costs are genuine, no doubt, little question as manufacturers of medicines would not price themselves out of business when their success is dependent on not only past successes, but future successes as well. In other words, medicines are usually rationally priced contrary to hysteria the public is fed. There are exceptions, marked exceptions to which courts of law ultimately attend. Cost controls and price manipulations by government are a fool's errand. The costs are simply what the costs are, and any governmental promise to lower them is a false promise. Somehow, some way, someone else will have to share or bear the cost to make up the difference.

Costs for research need to be recovered in order for new research to continue. Yet at base, high science comes with a high price tag. This is true of all of mankind's advancements. Scale may save, but advancements cost. The cost curve is geometric, not linear, and the government simply cannot change that. To use cost as a political tool does not foster the interests of anyone but for those who dwell in the shadows of politics continuously claiming victory, another partner of venality.

Free markets are still the best lid. If there are those who need help, then help them and assist them to again regain their footing.

Blaming hospitals, health care providers, the medical research companies, or whatever whipping boy politicians or their media partners choses to attack who provide and bring these lifesaving and life extending therapies, devices and medications to market is fruitless if not counterproductive. They can be not only genuinely expensive, but costs will continue to rise at rate far beyond the rise of the national economy. It is this technological tangential cost curve that is racing toward an economic plague, so to speak, a plague in the sense that it will financially overcome need. With it will come a new era of therapeutics.

If cost is burdensome now, it will be worse tomorrow, and more so the tomorrow after that until eschatological forces bring about collapse, or rationed based triage care becomes the law, the results of either being the same, visiting on some the same fate, not everyone will get treated. However, no worries, courts will surely get a swing at who gets to die (and who gets to live), and in either case perhaps even how. Please forgive me, but this is the nation you are inheriting, Pilgrim.

The endpoint is where for everyone the art and science of medicine simply cannot be afforded by even the government. Get used to it and get yourself mentally and emotionally ready. However, there is an end result, or shall we say a solution. Ultimately, the issue will come down to technology versus some value set, the ethics and values of the great and longstanding traditions of mankind, or at least America of yore, versus, say, *economic* reality. It will effectively be a colossal battle of institutions, corporeal and incorporeal.

The question is coming, and it will have to be dealt with, as is often the case, on the brink of disaster, maybe in the crucible of collapse or arising out of great ferment, or plague. Where will these matters be resolved? Congress will not get caught up in this political swamp. SCOTUS likewise, at least if it has learned its lesson to not poke its finger through a hole in the sociological wall, but instead wait until a new statute or rule is brought before it and then limit its decision to its constitutionality with perhaps a little *dicta* thrown in, which it is wont to do.

It is a challenge to discern whether government (the elected office holders) has failed the governed or the governed have failed the government as presumedly the governed have voted into office those who are representing them and running the show.

*

    The largest single cause of all pathologies is obesity*. Thirty to forty percent of the population is obese while over seventy per cent is overweight, and the numbers continue to climb. It is this problem of morbid excess weight which is behind not just diabetes (denominated as Type II), but the prime etiology of hypertension, heart disease, cerebral accidents (strokes), joint diseases, a bouquet of cancers, and galloping [as it were] depression [and its ever-present pathological twin, anxiety], presenting not just alone but commonly along with its many sequela. It is causative of most premature deaths and a catalogue of lingering chronic pathologies. It has an overwhelming effect on the health care system. Pathogenic obesity is now surpassing fifty per cent in some population communities. It is presenting a serious financial crisis. Much of the population is improperly eating its way into welfare lines and the health care system into bankruptcy. Most people will die an early death of obesity related diseases. Yet, most obesity is preventable or may be reversed.

*

    Every physician is now an obesity doctor. The surgeon must attend to complications related to obesity. The oncologist must attend to obesity. The cardiologist must attend to obesity. The pediatrician, the orthopedic physician, the endocrinologist, the family doctor, all are saddled with this seemingly passive but problematic pathology. Half the population now bellies up to the examination table for medical services related to not just their obesity, but a litany of other related self-inflicted pathologies, sequelae of every kind imaginable. Maybe Congress should legislate some discipline or regulate the people back to health? Wait, no. Votes, you understand. Then there are the health care and fast-food lobbies, neither of which seem to be inclined to help. Business is business. You probably do not like that. It is true.

While obesity is a self-inflicted condition which all of us pay for, yet in the overwhelming majority of cases it is all preventable or treatable without medicine.

*

Ethnicity and heritability may be factors in the onset of diabetes* (there are at least three types), but morbid obesity is by far the most common antecedent. Even where there may be a hereditary link in the development of diabetes, even then its etiology and manifestations are found in what and how much the 'victim' eats.

The most common and successful therapy is dietary management, or rather it should be. In the real world of medical practice, prescription drugs are the most common therapeutic employed as the discipline needed for 'dietary management' is simply beyond the ability of the great majority of patients. They cannot resist the temptation of excessively consuming 'foods' which are killing them, or down deep they simply do not care enough to control themselves. The necessary combination of character, discipline and motivation are simply not there. Particularly motivation. They would rather take a pill to manage it while continuing to partake in their dietary pleasures instead of following a regimen of good nourishment, exercise and rest as pathways back to health without regard for the price which they will ultimately pay, an expensive, early and harsh death following an unhappy, embarrassing and uncomfortable life.

One might wonder why drug companies are not required to include in their advertisements of medicines for the treatment of diabetes the proper natural way back to health along with an explanation associated with the miracle drug they have developed, which again all of us pay for one way or another. Cigarette manufacturers, another drug company, must do so. It has helped. Why the difference in legal treatment of the issue?

Diabetes is presented here as being overall among the most common and costliest of all chronic pathologies. It is among the largest drains on health care resources, and *most* of it is avoidable. Like obesity [the costliest disease] it is typically self-inflicted. It now effects over fifty million residents of the United States, is alarmingly increasing with the prediabetes population now coming in at over fifty percent. Obesity and diabetes are clearly epidemics, nigh pandemics, putting it mildly. You would think the government would declare a crisis. It hasn't. Why not?

What is government doing about these diseases? Nothing significant. The medical establishment? Nothing meaningful. Why? Votes and profits get in the way. No? All truth is spoken through behavior.

*

A cure for cancer has been found!? The reality of the matter is there is no one disease of 'cancer.' It is rather a broad spectrum of diseases, a constellation of pathologies often profoundly different from one another as well as how they respond to a myriad of therapies, if at all, as well as what their etiologies may be. Treatments may vary, but the closest common denominator of its etiology is a failure of the immune system which itself is also a sequela to obesity.

Failure of the immune system and the body's inability to heal itself or repair diseased tissues generally accounts for more 'cancers' than do the oceans of carcinogens in which we all live. Lifestyles can compromise the immune system. Yet, even what would otherwise be overwhelming waves of carcinogens may not defeat an otherwise robust immune response. At the same time the propensity for the development of cancer may be an inherited trait which is now being scientifically addressed [See: genome research, *infra*].

In most cases apart from heritability, the victim has weakened himself; diet, inactivity, alcohol, smoking, and obesity all being among the leading culprits, primarily obesity. In other words, in large measure people are responsible for their own cancers outside of any genetic and/or congenital succession.

Trillions, not millions, not billions, trillions of dollars have been thrown at research and the quest for a 'cure.' The efficacy of this spending has been disappointing as compared with other areas of science in terms of wide spectrum success. It has historically been a black hole. 'Cure rates' have often been measured in terms of life extensions (typically two to five years) with remissions being overall relatively low.

In the midst of all of this are 'health' related organizations which advertise their life saving or life extending capabilities capitalizing on the weaknesses of the hopeless. Loathsome to say the least, but reflective of the corrupting influence of money in the land of the vulnerable customer who is in a world of despair.

At the same time, finally, there have been some recent areas of genuine and significant progress often with spectacular results. Many past therapies are now coming to be looked upon as barbaric and foolish as bloodletting and trephining as treatment advances unfold. At the same time, disappointments abound when considering the government's declaration of 'war on cancer' more than half a century ago, even being a plank in a presidential election platform.

On balance, it now comes down to early detection being best coupled with the emerging availability of several genuine cures. However, as irony would have it, there will be some unforeseen consequences.

There is no doubt early detection of the disease is often the *sine qua non* for a road back to health. But it is the rapidly rising cost of newly developed cures which is the emerging problem. Overall, the current cost-benefit ratios in many cases will look something like more than a million dollars per patient, if not per patient-year. This calculus will be taken into consideration where unfortunately so many will ultimately die anyway and often being pharmacologically incapacitated in the meantime. Thus, it is obvious where this is headed.

Emerging exceptions to the hopelessness of a cancer diagnosis in the recent past have put the powerful effects of the random ratio of reinforcement paradigm into play driving research to new break throughs. Bright spots which are emerging wouldn't exist without this Herculean effort. The relatively recent event of the opening of the genetic codes is now and will continue to be leading the major advances in charting courses of treatments and cures focused on helping the body to heal and repair itself at the cellular level by revitalizing the immune system. Science *is* on the brink.

*

Cures will come with a seismic economic impact. The Social Security retirement programs [along with its benefit counterparts] will suffer a nearly instantaneous actuarial default in anticipation of being unable to fund itself in the very short term. Public and private pensions will also snap under the weight of life expectancy being extended another ten years, just to guess a number. Everything in the realm of healthcare, end of life therapies and treatment decisions will come to be fenced in by an unwelcomed explosion in costs and ultimately the need for rationing. Healthcare protocols will have to be revised setting up standards for who will be treated, how they will be treated, and even if they will be treated. Moreover, the nation's social support system, already starting to teeter, is presently becoming even more top heavy with oldsters which a cure will dramatically exacerbate.

*

What is Congress going to do? Nothing. Bad for business. It probably will not touch it. If it does decide to act, it will surely figure out a way to make it worse. How about putting in place a politically insulating commission?

The underlying problem? There simply will not be sufficient resources of every kind to go around. Human services and financial capacity will be overwhelmed. Medical costs of the new science will strip budgets which will ultimately collapse.

Next step? Triage. That would be rationing. [It will be interesting to see what new name for rationing politicians will come up with to make it more 'palatable.' Maybe Department of Life Choices?] Triage by whom? Bureaucrats? Elected officials? Most likely it will start with a congressionally appointed committee, if Congress decides to act, a 'citizen's blue-ribbon commission', of course. Congress will not act by itself, naturally. Then there will be panels created, 'citizens panels,' in fact a series of panels for every county, community parish and borough selected in pretty much the same way all other appointed positions are handled by government. They will decide who gets what therapies and who gets to die.

*

Then somewhere, sometime, someone is going to file a lawsuit. Some gutsy, bright lawyer will step up to the plate with the case hopefully assigned to a gutsy, hardworking, thoughtful, unbiased judge. Now the judicial process can look at 'fair play and substantial justice, be he prince or pauper,' 'the conscience of the people,' 'deep-seated traditions,' and do what Congress or the Executive Branch of government has failed or refused to do. It will make a judicial review of what the appointees may have botched. Why? Because there is precedent. The High Court has been known to act in the face of legislative malaise and write the law itself. It also has experience in the department of who gets to live and who gets to die [*Roe* and Washington v. Glucksberg, 521 U. S. 702*].

This could happen in 2024. If not, it is nevertheless coming, a cure followed by an overwhelmed health care system followed by economically driven rationing. All are presently on the horizon and there is anthropological precedent for what is done with oldsters nearing the end of life, or the incurable.

Why not become a Lawyer and a Doctor, Pilgrim?

IX

SEX AND GENDER

The subject of human sex has been a perennial crowd pleaser for all of recorded history, and likely from the first appearance of the specie given its success. In this instance, the word 'sex' is being used as a verb. In spite of the fact the terms sex and gender are often used interchangeably, they are not. They are starkly different.

What follows is based on four decades of longitudinal research over a series of lateral cohorts of individual groups accumulating data from thousands of students and patients. No opinions are offered, only a rhetorical report of that collective data and the ancillary findings to which it speaks. Universities and clinics provide living laboratories, a once in a lifetime opportunity to research issues hiding in plain sight. The universities also provide an unmatched inventories of otherwise unavailable information and useful knowledge apart from curricula.

Without getting too far into the weeds, let us agree on usage. For our purposes, the term 'sex' is a biological term of art [without reference to its use as a verb], and the term 'gender' as an emotional term of art [for now without reference to its many behavioral counterparts], or in a more encompassing sense, psychological in character. The former is a status defined physiologically and assigned at birth whereas the latter is a condition experienced at the emotional level ultimately manifested through behavior or behavioral choices.

As will become apparent, there are gradations within both sex and gender. Although typically fairly standard and stable, each can manifest remarkable variations. Furthermore, although their covariance is typically direct, this is not always the case and indeed can manifest indirect covariance over a wide, dramatic and colorful spectrum of presentations, albeit a relatively rare phenomenon.

Also brought into play are issues of psychological degrees of gender ['genderness' if you will] alongside the biological concept of degrees of 'masculinity' and 'femininity' both in the context of everything from athletics to personal relationships, science to art, and needless to say, that ubiquitous social quagmire of 'personal choices.' Are there any legal issues here? Athletics, perhaps to probably. Education, likely. Personal relationships? Not so much, at least for now.

In this general arena and also added to the usual dyadic classifications of sex and gender are the LGBT, LGBTQ+ or LGBTQIA, etc., stable of categories. Thus, we now seemingly have several genders, which can be mixed according to some authorities, or no gender at all [or so say those who make a living heralding change, particularly in academia], or do we? Some observers contend that youth receive influential 'social adjusting,' or social direction during their formative or developmental years. Others contend one is dealt a 'genetic hand' at conception which dictates all bio-behavioral aspects of life from that moment on.

Scientifically, as well as socially, it is not as simple as that. Recognition and incipient acceptance of new classifications? It's here, but still much veiled. Facilities and accommodations of all kinds, separate or generic? They are appearing. New and/or separate classifications, each with an emerging tailored legal status, and a new *corpus juris*, so to speak? Well, yes, at least in terms of protection if not validation. Who will ultimately decide their legitimacy? The Supreme Court I suppose, unless of course it dawns on Congress that a measurable segment of the population is represented here [possibly one or two percent, more or less depending on the authority one chooses to rely upon, and perhaps even far more as recognized on the Biobehavioral Genderesque Matrix, *infra*, if you choose to allow your thinking to reside on a continuum]. Legislative responses to such issues could be politically advisable [think votes]. On the other hand, the response of offended voters could be costly. Out trot the pollsters and demographers.

However, before going there, let us examine what is actually before us in this regard. It may be looked upon as a frank medical matter, or to put it less pejoratively, a biological matter. For some, a psychiatric issue. There are also those who would say, or at least pitch it as being an environmental matter, or socially and/or experientially based, etiologically speaking. But does that make a real difference?

Check your sensitivities at the door. Regardless how one feels, what *is* before us is a highly affectable matter calling for a delicate examination. It is a fact of life unbound by time or place. It does impact citizens' rights, which in some countries would be an understatement, and always has been. Societal perspectives have been varied to put it in the mildest of terms.

*

Let us perform a mental abstraction on the black board of our minds unfettered by notions of the perennial right/wrong dichotomy and polemics which flow from them since we dwell above such tauromachy. Therefore, visualize two circles of equal size, side by side. Let us label the one on the left "male" and the one on the right "female." This is traditionally how the world has seen sex as well as gender. The fact is this male/female absolute dyad is not even close to what on occasion actually exists, clinically and/or socially. Furthermore, both of the two variables [gender and sex] are themselves on a curve. These curves are typically in covariance but might to some degree on occasion be independent of one another, that is they do not always harmoniously match. And now the fight breaks out.

Slide the two circles over and partially upon one another until they overlap so that the outer circumference of each one passes through the center point of the other circle leaving substantially more than fifty percent of each circle exposed as being uncovered on each side, and substantially less than fifty percent of the area of two circles in the overlapped position now in the center, eclipsed if you will (each eclipsing the other). In reality the overlap could be more or less. Clinicians might not be in agreement as to percentages, but for purposes of this discussion, the relationship described is sufficient to illustrate the point to be made. Those without an agenda would likely see the degree of significant overlap as being much smaller. Those with an agenda will claim it to be more. That is fine. Differences in degree nevertheless support and recognize the existence of the commonality of the underlying concept, which is explained as we proceed.

Next, place the centers of these two partially overlapped side by side circles on the axis of the horizontal coordinate (the x-axis or abscissa), half of each circle above the line and half of each circle below, and the geographic center of the two combined and overlapped circles over the vertical coordinate (the y-axis or ordinate), half of the overlapped circles' areas to the left and half to the right, each coordinate splitting down the middle both horizontally and vertically.

The x-axis represents 'degree of sexuality' in terms of masculinity and femininity (a biological construct). The y-axis represents 'behavioral expression' and sense of self arising out of inner emotional feelings of maleness or femaleness (a psychological construct [in today's new world, degree or kind of genderness as some current thought now embraces]).

As can be readily seen, the possibilities, for practical purposes, are nigh infinite. Now we have started to demonstrate a better or at least more expansive conception of 'gender' as some might countenance today. In other words, gender is far from being an 'absolute' in any sense of degree or manifestation and is in fact very much on what has turned out to be part of multivariate curves (or of degrees). This paradigm represents a constellation of infinite variables. It is referred to as the Biobehavioral Genderesque Matrix [BGM].

Let us disabuse ourselves of the idea that genders are absolutely bimodally discrete, the term binary being commonly used historically. In other words, gender is also on a continuum, again referred to here as a curve. To further charge the issue, gender is now being more and more viewed, understood and accepted as being separate from biological sex traditionally assigned at birth based on physiology. If you like this you are going to love the biological aspects of sex, itself also being on a curve, at least this is what science is now telling us. Impossible, right? Let us take a look.

What can be said about these overlapped two circles is there are those who would find themselves in the un-eclipsed portion of their respective areas, male or female. That is to say, those who find themselves in much of the unmasked portion of either the male or female circles would be viewed in today's sense as being for practical purposes fully or at least substantially biologically male or female, while still recognizing degrees of prominence. At the extremes, left and right, one might observe another as being the personification of masculinity or femininity [setting aside the invalidating influences of political correctness].

In the middle, the eclipsed portions of the two circles, reposes a blend. Notice, however, that it shades from one side to the other with women becoming less feminine as we move to the left of their orbit and men becoming less masculine as we move to the right of theirs. Or put otherwise, as we move from left of center to the western most limits of the eclipsed female portion of the diagram, the more masculinized our female is. And, likewise, the reciprocal for the male who finds himself on the eastern most parts of the male overlap being a more feminized male. Know that this has nothing to do with who as human beings they may be. Masculinized women tend to be.... Feminized men tend to be.... So far as genderness is concerned (behavioral and psychological), the same variables can be identified and assigned up and down the y axis, $+y$ for masculine, $-y$ for feminine if you will, or the other way around if that is more comfortable for you.

The reciprocals and blends are myriad. The possibilities are veritably infinite. It is our world. We see it around us. It is readily observable. While we know it is there it has substantially gone undiscussed until recently, simply unreported much to the consternation of some, though it need not be.

In the central *region* along the x axis of 'sexuality' (biologically speaking), and the 'sense of gender' along the y axis, the most 'gender confusion' is likely to be observed or experienced [See: Revised DSM-5TR (Diagnostic and Statistical Manuel published by the American Psychiatric Association): Gender Dysphoria*], but not exclusively, nor always. To reduce this to a simple explanatory sentence, regardless of our anatomy (which itself is not always manifested in frank and discrete physiological expressions sexually, data and metrics of which are presently being developed without much fanfare rather understandably), the human species ranges from males being very masculine to being very effeminate, and females who are very feminine to very masculine. Many of the males on this curve (in the penumbra of the overlap) are more feminine than many females, and reciprocally with females who are more masculine than many males, again a readily observable fact. This is not common, but it happens. Anatomically they typically fall into clearer biological classifications with regard to sex assigned at birth, but not always.

From the clinical perspective of sex, cases of doubt are rare. When they occur, they are classified as a 'sexual differentiation disorder*.' Frank hermaphroditism as an observed perinatal genetic error, is very rare. Overall intersex* rates are put by the NIH [National Institute of Health] at 0.018%. Advocacy groups often come in much higher, some approaching 100 times more which puts it at 1+%. Its psychological and/or behavioral counterpart and its many variants might be subsumed under 'gender confusion' or Gender Dysphoria in DSM speak, assuming it arises to a level of consciousness.

In the BGM, it is the amount of overlap which can be startling. No one seems to want to look. Our social inclination has been to turn a blind eye as being what one might suppose to be the politically correct or socially comfortable thing to do, at least until recently. It seems to have been historically all but unmentionable or at least simply unnecessary to mention. Tie this to the fact that on occasion, as indicated in the BGM, gender (the emotional sense of who one is as a personal subjective matter) and sex (who one is biologically) do not match up as ordinarily expected sets up a situation from which emerges or may emerge clinically frank diagnosable Gender Dysphoria. At the same time there are a few who are simply innately unhappy with who they are and use this 'incongruence' as an escape if not a distraction.

*

It was once fashionable for some to refer to people who tended to cluster in the center, be they male or female by assignment or some other bio-behavioral qualification, as "androgynous," and all was well and good. It had a sort of complimentary character, at least for a while. Descriptive terms for those within their gender category but featuring enduring traits from across genderosexual lines were often not as complimentary. Androgynous? Okay. Much of anything else, not so good. Following a brief social period, eventually even the mild moniker androgynous was not received pleasantly by most, particularly men, many of whom seemed not to have a proclivity to be either female or reflect femaleness. It may have seemed palliative to the other party, the oftentimes speaker, usually because it was perceived to be if not self-elevating in some circles at least a leveling term, if not a frank attempt to check. It has now all but disappeared.

The 'why' side of the vicissitudes of androgyny, however, has escaped many scientists, or so the paucity of reported studies would suggest [read politically selected for publication]. Maybe it is a sociopolitical anathema simply to be avoided, ignored or buried, a common tactic also among academics as with the elected and politically ensconced. The fact is as 'androgyny' came into the marketplace of ideas it was lighted upon for seemingly sociopolitical reasons, and a new prong in the era of gender politics began. A new description and category of "equality" began to emerge, along with the embryonic struggle for sameness, as it were, being off-and-on quite popular. It opened the door to a new status which was going to be politically acceptable for some, leading to the opening of doors to other thematic variables which in time would also become politically acceptable. And here we are. In other words (fast forward to today, or tomorrow), to think there is only the male, female, or even homosexual as categories is simply not the case. These are the facts biologically, and now emerging more publicly behaviorally, although still struggling legally while perhaps currently enjoying favored status politically, at least this appears to be the present 'zeitgeist for some,' admittedly an oxymoron.

As has been said, there are multivariate expressions both physiologically resting along the abscissa (the horizontal coordinate) as well as behaviorally resting along the ordinate (the vertical coordinate), constituting florid variations within the paradigm of the Biobehavioral Genderesque Matrix, far beyond the basic and rigid male/female dichotomy. In this abscissa-ordinate display one will witness a multi-dimensional presentation of colorfully different constellations of transsexual behaviors to orientation confusion, a myriad of sexual preferences (far outside 'yesterday's' male-female dyad), to asexuality or the once embraced homosexual 'triad,' and far beyond, *ad infinitum*. We are no longer a society, or species, of just male and female, at least so far as some of the current social order is now concerned. Quite to the contrary, unlike virtually all the rest of the animal kingdom, or life forms of any kind, we are now holding ourselves out to be a panoply of *gendere differentia* with variations far beyond the brief outline presented here, at least so goes the public discourse.

Social forces influence the outward or genderesque expression of these biological variations, provoking some to exhibit behavioral traits, suppressing others, but with the underlying systemics remaining intact, at least that is what we have been told. No one has performed an adequate study of the effects of parents and parenting skills or social pressures, or the absence thereof as they relate to the issue of gender confusion, gender dysphoria and its sequela as has been done with, to pick one social concern, crime. It would make for a great dissertation or research paper, but be careful, such things can get you fired, flunked out of your program, or cancelled altogether if you cross the line of the popular narrative.

Affectivity (inner feelings or sense of self) and gender self-identification and their related behaviors are correlative and reflective (harmonizing) matters. At the same time, readily observable indications suggest they are frankly biological phenomena in etiology, inherited traits, at least according to the scientific test of markers being present *ab initio*, incipient developmentally, refractory to change and stable over time, in fact fairly stable through all recorded history in character, incidence, prevalence and persistence. That seals the issue for scientists. Or put this way, such markers and their permanency as indicated suggest all of this is therefore biologically based, or 'genetic' if you prefer. This, of course, is a matter of rabid debate far from resolution. The fact is, however, people know who they are and they know it early on. All you have to do is to ask them. They may be reticent, but they will eventually speak. Even if they do not answer when asked they will speak via their behaviors. The one person they can never fool is themselves.

Not one scientific study has even demonstrated or even successfully suggested that gender (or sexual preferences) has been or is permanently influenced by environmental factors or by influences *dehors* the organism. It is frankly biological, a feature like any other difference in humanity. It is not subject to judgment or choice any more than height or weight, talent or intellect, color or form. As with temperament and personality structures which flow therefrom, it is all inherited.

Although prevalence rates have been debated, different positions taken tend to reflect points of politics, sociological polemics and disputation, or attitudes apart from points of science. Add to this is the emergence of trans or pangenderism, neutrois, nonbinary, gender fluidity or asexuality racing through the entire constellation of human existence now being collectively denominated by, *inter alia*, neopronouns such as "Ze."

*

The 'why' side of all of this is one of the challenges to which valid and reliable evidence is still being gathered. Current thought with regard to frank biobehavioral aberrations now includes the possibility of a fracture or unexpected appearance of an allele in the chromosomal array, or a random or accidental paring, or possibly environmental mutating influences on the epigenome or the epigenetic 'laboratory.' Add to all of this the notion that gender is on a curve, and the whole matter becomes provoking to even ponder let alone organize and isolate for scientific study, but unbiased studies are beginning to emerge. The perennial problem is, of course, which ones will get published. So far as the law is concerned --- hold your breath --- the Supreme Court may eventually have to speak.

*

The message? Live your life. Play the hand you were dealt. Be yourself. Do what brings you peace and happiness. This might not please everyone, but no one pleases everyone. You will never be happy trying to make everyone else happy. Do not try to fool yourself or anyone else. Be gentle and respectful. Don't be led by the noise. Be part of your community and participate in it. Serve when needed. Capitalize on the gifts you have been given. It's your life. Live it well. If you do this you will be happy, satisfied, contented and at peace. In other words, your life will be successful.

Capiche, Pilgrim?

X

POPULATION

The world's population is exploding, but this garners no serious attention, or at this point we as a nation apparently no longer care. Maybe it has fallen victim to social or media exhaustion. Where do you read or see that nearly one fourth of the world's population is undernourished, hungry? Hundreds of thousands if not millions are murdered every year. Extermination is occurring. Slaves are being worked to early deaths. Yet populations continue to balloon. Where is the media? Why is it not reported?

Millions upon millions are flooding across the borders into the United States in multiples over the current birth rate. This flooding is bringing in the uneducated, unskilled, often morbid, many being felons and terrorists from every corner of the world. They are without knowledge or spirit of American civics and values, many even anti-American now being more and more representative of the populace, a disparate and separated class. They are not material for any pillar of society, but particularly an informed citizenry and electorate needed to keep a Republic and willing to put country ahead of self when necessary.

The exploding illegal migrant population has not garnered the attention it deserves given the consequences which will be following. It hasn't, but it will. For some reason and for now this explosion has become, "this is just healthy growth," or "we need them in the fields," etc., invention after invention. All the while the government is putting the interests of these illegal entries ahead of not only those seeking to enter legally, but the nation's children in need, veterans, the unfortunate.

How fast the public forgets, and politicians know it, so too the media. Again, one invention to another. But what happens when the nation experiences the next swing of the natural business cycle? Will they displace the citizens 'above' them who will be the ones now to lose *their* jobs and default on *their* debts? This is what you are inheriting, and it also will not be good.

The fact is the population was half its present size only two generations ago. The problem is that a growing number and percentage of the population are not worthy let alone capable of being responsible citizens. They are too often detached and unconcerned, criminals, mentally ill, or worse. Further, it is likely most will not contribute to the national fisc, but rather be a heavy burden. Worst of all, most will not become Americans even if they gain some form of citizenship.

As the nation is being overrun, it is also being overcome by self-inflicted pathologies and economic sinkholes of every description, along with the morbidly obese and its sequela packing into waiting rooms. The tab is not just running up but is out of control. You will be paying for it along with supporting the uneducated, the undereducated, the unmotivated, the careless, the malnourished, the hapless new neighbor who forgot to use a government issued condom, all of them, separately and collectively, with losses from rampant crime capping it all.

If the economics are allowed to play out in accordance with its present trajectory, you will be working less for yourself than for others, or so say the numbers. But certainly any politician worth his/her salt is going to say that isn't so, or, it can be made up, it can be worked out, do a little more deficit spending here and a little there which also costs citizens even though it is nearly invisible as it shrinks whatever present wage or salary happens to be paid in terms of real spending power leaving the worker with perhaps the same dollar count but now worth less. Who among your friends and neighbors are recognizing this, and which of your politicians are warning you? Higher and higher taxes and the Dollar being shrunk by deficit spending reduces the value of your work. It is in fact a 'taking' from you. Perhaps disguised, but nevertheless a taking. As it stands, it will not just continue, but accelerate. Hopefully someday, somewhere, some lawyer is going to fight this even if at a horrible personal expense.

Maybe make some changes, there are happy days just ahead, we just need to keep our spirits up, we are gaining on it, and hope fiercely we are told. Not just fools, but damnable fools. As you think about this, remember that the media supports political attacks and character assassinative 'reporting.' They are the propaganda arm for the politics of their choice. Political reporting need not be truthful, and it isn't. It is misleading, abusive and destructive. [Remember the gift from SCOTUS, New York Times v. Sullivan, 376 U. S. 254*?]

*

Your government *is* transforming your country, Pilgrim.

XI

WW III

A final scenario, Pilgrim, which is coming to your neighborhood, and this how it will unfold. The President is faced with eminent nuclear strikes against the United States; harbors will be lost, carriers [America's 'Maginot Line*'] will be evaporated, cities gone, the seats of government leveled, lines of communication severed, basic resources and supplies, assets of every kind, lost, and maybe even the will to resist. All will be lost in a flash or series of flashes [all out global war on the highest order will now be decided in a matter of hours if not minutes…, not years]. There will be no period for arsenals of democracy to build anything let alone building goods for war. As matters are presently set, any dithering will be fatal.

What is left of the citizenry will be cast into sheer despair and utter destitution. Animal behaviors will emerge. Eventually this will be followed by men organizing those who are left into 'local' governments, everyone essentially becoming first responders, the indomitable spirit of humans struggling to preserve as much of their lives and themselves as they are able. Those few who know what to do will lead. The others will wisely stay close by. History and models of science have demonstrated this survival phenomenon over and over, again and again.

Perhaps you may think you know what war is like. You do not. You cannot even imagine it. Again, what you see in the movies, on television, the internet, your apps, do not even come close to capturing what goes on; the stink and unwashable stench, the deafening cacophony of chaotic shots and explosions, tremors racing across the earth, blood, guts, brains and cries everywhere all bathed in filth, suffering, intractable fear and panic, a pink mist of exploding bodies, death everywhere, and today being incinerated, flash after flash. The population will be reduced to a hoard of wild animals wearing rags, carrying guns, taking what they want, indiscriminate savagery of the ugliest and most unimaginable order.

I shall not try to paint the grim picture as it cannot be truly painted. Once upon us, it will have to wring itself out. If you think back, no one imagined, nor could they even imagine a 9/11 event [a prick compared to what is coming] as it was simply unimaginable not just by you but everyone you know along with the 'intelligence' services and the supposed security forces. It was beyond comprehension, simply not in one's bank of understanding let alone anticipation, and therefore went unforeseen, but now carries with it an important lesson. What is unimaginable now *is* coming from forces external, then internal, in devastation of the entire nation, your nation. You say impossible? Not. Agony and despair will not even come close to describing what the nation will experience.

As it will turn out, intelligence services have made it clear that not only are plans for attacking the United States complete and means operationally developed along with the process of delivery being now available (until recently the missing link ---- the old 'cold war' posed less of a threat than was publicly believed for that reason alone) and is about to be initiated. There is little if any doubt, or as it is often cast, beyond any reasonable doubt.

Foreign adversaries care nothing about life. They are sociopathicly devoid of any feelings for others or even their own nation's population. They are insensitive to life. It is only the state which matters. That is difficult to imagine because it is a cultural issue.

Might a pusillanimous President refuse to act and instead order the Attorney General to file an original action with the Supreme Court in a blame shifting maneuver as politicians do [hoping to avoiding being 'hung by the heels*' from a lamppost on the National Mall] seeking a declaratory judgment as to the legality of the classified proposed response prepared by the Joint Chiefs to this real and imminent threat, a pre-emptive nuclear strike of overwhelming proportions expected to effectively reduce the military of the would-be aggressing nations to waste. Or will this nation simply cease to exist because of cowardice and/or incompetent delay?

That depends on who is President. In fact, the Constitution was drafted so as to give the power to the President to act as necessary *instanter* in circumstances such as this, circumstances of a clear and present national peril, eminent danger of destruction. Indeed, one who accepts the office must swear to act accordingly. Choose your leaders carefully, Pilgrim.

The positions of the nation's enemies, their military personnel and weaponry, their leadership all have been programmed into ballistic and cruise missiles ready for delivery as well as other laser and guided ordnance, part of the land, sea, and air triad plus orbiting assets including e-weaponry, and ready for launch. The enemy threat can be effectively annihilated. If struck first, the United States will suffer the same fate. The President has been advised by the Joint Chiefs and the intelligence communities that the nation has but a matter of minutes to act.

What if the nation's leader is gutless and not willing to fight using whatever it takes to protect the American people, and win? What if the President is a fool or a political fraud? What if we have a leader who thinks we have it coming? What if the leader, contrary to all tactical advice, wants to negotiate, try to see it their way, exhaust all possible 'diplomatic' solutions first [suicidal under the exigent circumstances]?

If the United States is defeated [inconceivable, no?], all the nation's leaders, or what may be left of them, will surely be executed in the most unceremonious ways for war crimes attendant to last ditch and crippled retaliatory nuclear efforts to save themselves, no question, as would have been the case at the end of the Second World War for the use of atomic weapons had it turned out differently, which it almost did. If not, then at the hands of the people.

As irony would have it, or good luck, the use of nuclear weapons which ended WWII would have been seen as war crimes had matters turned out differently, yet this is what actually shortened the war and saved countless American lives. The Germans were closing in on developing a nuclear device and a Japanese Admiral made one miscalculation that ended any chance of victory in the Pacific. Few realize how close it was. Of course, these things do not get publicized, nor is it generally taught. It wouldn't be politically correct. Further, such history does not fit the present narrative. But what does that matter as history is now being rewritten or unwritten anyway?

"Let us try to see their point of view." Maybe we can change their minds? Shall we not try that first? "Let us go to diplomacy…, negotiate?" My God, the world is starting on fire! It is, right now. Look around and you will see the scenario in its incipient forms. The antecedents for WWIII are *now* underway right before our eyes. For some nations, make no mistake about it, it is already here. Major conflicts start insidiously, and then all of a sudden it is happening, always.

But the nation sleeps, the leaders are dithering in half measures, truth is being hidden or cancelled and the country is awash in propaganda. Read history. Think not that our adversaries are not watching as the President is piddling our way into global conflict. There *is* right now another 'gathering storm*.'

Cowardice, national decomposition, debt, the absence of statesmanship along with geopolitical negligence have historically ended in defeat. Compromised leaders cuts deep wounds..., betrayal is worse.

Without clearance from the High Court the President has informed the Joint Chiefs there will be no pre-emptive strike. He is afraid to make the decision and the risk of unpleasant personal consequences. Backwater contacts with key members of Congress have indicated there will be no help there, a not surprising revelation. Additionally, confidentiality would be out of the question as too many members have their own personal agendas; shallow, feckless, spineless, raised and elected in a world of engendered dependency. Many politicians aim to keep it that way and enrich themselves in the process. If one attempts to interfere, one will pay the price. Many are self-absorbed, narcissistic, born leakers, pathological liars putting self and agenda ahead of what is best for the country. Foot soldiers of the Constitution they are not and never will be. Perhaps that is another reason why, in the vision of the drafters of the Constitution the President was made commander in chief assuming, one would think, that whoever held the office would be from the same mold as those who founded the nation and have behind them an educated public. How could it be any other way?

The Chairman of the fourth branch then quietly but clearly indicated to the President that if no orders are immediately forthcoming, the President will be taken into protective custody (the Secret Service will pose no barrier) and removed to a safe location, and that he will personally lead a preemptive strike. It is known as duty, duty driven initiative, a concept understood by few, a concept no longer publicly taught let alone generally embraced.

An attempt to file suit is nevertheless elected. How will the Court rule? SCOTUS deciding a military matter? How could that be? How could it know? A body politic, again, made up of members who have never served, aren't serving, and never will serve so much as a day in harm's way. As with most other members of government, the Court is totally devoid of any military knowledge or experience as to how the military functions operationally, strategically, and/or tactically, what it can and cannot do and how quickly, now to decide a military question let alone a question of war relative to not just the security, but the very existence of the nation and the survival of its inhabitants? How can there even be jurisdiction here? There isn't. The Constitution put issue solely in the hands of the President as Commander in Chief.

Will the Four-Star act? That depends on who is wearing the four stars.

*

So, Pilgrim, you can see the nation needs you. What are you going to do?

Questions, Suggestions, Comments or Complaints?

I am truly interested in your thoughts.

<drclarkjohnson@law.msu.edu>

Milton Keynes UK
Ingram Content Group UK Ltd.
UKHW021934220724
5848UK00001B/48